Houghton Mifflin Harcourt
Modern Chemistry

Performance Expectations Guide

Houghton Mifflin Harcourt.

Contents

Performance Expectations Guide

Introduction

The Next Generation Science Standards (NGSS) include Performance Expectations for chemistry that state what you should know and be able to do by the end of the course. This guide provides activities to help you prepare to meet the standards.

For each Performance Expectation, you will find a Challenge Activity that is posed as a performance task—a lab or an investigation, a research project, or another activity. The task addresses the Performance Expectation. The Challenge Activity will provide some guidance, such as background information, materials to use, questions to consider, and tips for completing the challenge successfully.

Chemistry Performance Expectations

Matter and Its Interactions

HS-PS1-1   Use the periodic table as a model to predict the relative properties of elements based on the patterns of electrons in the outermost energy level of atoms.

HS-PS1-2   Construct and revise an explanation for the outcome of a simple chemical reaction based on the outermost electron states of atoms, trends in the periodic table, and knowledge of the patterns of chemical properties.

HS-PS1-3   Plan and conduct an investigation to gather evidence to compare the structure of substances at the bulk scale to infer the strength of electrical forces between particles.

HS-PS1-4   Develop a model to illustrate that the release or absorption of energy from a chemical reaction system depends upon the changes in total bond energy.

HS-PS1-5   Apply scientific principles and evidence to provide an explanation about the effects of changing the temperature or concentration of the reacting particles on the rate at which a reaction occurs.

HS-PS1-6   Refine the design of a chemical system by specifying a change in conditions that would produce increased amounts of products at equilibrium.*

HS-PS1-7   Use mathematical representations to support the claim that atoms, and therefore mass, are conserved during a chemical reaction.

HS-PS1-8   Develop models to illustrate the changes in the composition of the nucleus of the atom and the energy released during the processes of fission, fusion, and radioactive decay.

Motion and Stability: Forces and Interactions

HS-PS2-6   Communicate scientific and technical information about why the molecular-level structure is important in the functioning of designed materials.*

Engineering Design

HS-ETS1-1 Analyze a major global challenge to specify qualitative and quantitative criteria and constraints for solutions that account for societal needs and wants.

HS-ETS1-2 Design a solution to a complex real-world problem by breaking it down into smaller, more manageable problems that can be solved through engineering.

HS-ETS1-3 Evaluate a solution to a complex real-world problem based on prioritized criteria and tradeoffs that account for a range of constraints, including cost, safety, reliability, and aesthetics, as well as possible social, cultural, and environmental impacts.

HS-ETS1-4 Use a computer simulation to model the impact of proposed solutions to a complex real-world problem with numerous criteria and constraints on interactions within and between systems relevant to the problem.

*denotes the integration of traditional science content with an engineering practice

HS-PS1-1: Using the Periodic Table

HS-PS1-1 Use the periodic table as a model to predict the relative properties of elements based on the patterns of electrons in the outermost energy level of atoms.

Challenge Activity

Challenge: Predict the properties of elements by their positions in the periodic table.

The most amazing thing about the periodic table is that chemists conceived of it before they had any idea atoms contained electrons or, for that matter, were entirely convinced atoms themselves even existed. What led them to the discovery was the simple yet powerful observation that elements could be categorized according to their chemical properties and that these properties appeared to vary in a predictable way as atomic mass increased. The patterns seemed so obvious that Dmitri Mendeleev, the Russian chemist most often credited with drawing up the first periodic table, even felt confident in predicting the existence of unknown elements simply to keep the patterns of properties intact. His predictions proved correct.

The shape of the modern periodic table is a result of how electrons fill the energy levels of the atoms of the elements contained in it. As you can see below, there are seven rows, called periods, in the periodic table. Not coincidentally, there are seven main energy levels electrons can occupy around an atom. The elements are arranged by increasing atomic number, and those elements whose outer electrons occupy one of the main energy levels are placed in rows on top of one another. Elements in columns have similar chemical properties—the patterns noticed by Mendeleev and other chemists of the past. These vertical columns are known as groups. What makes the properties of the elements in groups similar is that these elements have a similar outer electron configuration.

In this activity, look for and describe any patterns you can see in the properties of the elements in the periodic table. Describe how these patterns depend on the outermost electrons of the atoms of those elements. By the end of the activity, you should be able to describe the properties of any given element in relation to any other element.

MATERIALS

- appropriate reference materials
- periodic table listing element symbols, element names, atomic numbers, and atomic masses
- periodic tables listing any of the following: atomic radii, ionic radii, ionization energy, electron affinity, electronegativity, or any other property

MEET THE CHALLENGE

1. Look at several periodic tables and examine the information contained in each.

2. Consider how values for various properties (such as atomic radius, ionization energy, and electron affinity) increase or decrease as you move from right to left, up and down, and even diagonally along the table.

3. Draw a conclusion about how the values change. For example, you might say "[Property] increases as you move up and to the right along the table."

4. Consider what changes about the electron configuration of the elements. For example, you might say "As [property] increases as you move to the right on the periodic table, the number of outermost electrons increases."

5. In groups of two or larger, challenge one another to predict relative element properties. For example, if given the element boron, you could say, "Boron has an ionization energy greater than [other element] but less than [other element]."

TIPS

- The properties of the elements in the periodic table follow *general* trends. Do not be surprised if you see values for properties that do not follow the trends exactly.

- Concentrate on outer electrons and how atomic number relates to the number of electrons in the outer energy levels of atoms.

- Try graphing values of element properties by atomic number. Even a simple graph sometimes can make changes more evident.

- Don't be concerned with being able to provide exact values when making comparisons. The point of the activity is to understand how the properties of elements compare in a *relative* way. For example, understanding that the ionization energy for cobalt is higher than it is for potassium but lower than it is for bromine is sufficient.

DOCUMENTATION

1. Provide evidence that you understand how the periodic table can be used as a model to predict the relative properties of elements based on the patterns of electrons in the outermost energy level of atoms.

2. **Visual** Draw a picture or construct a graph:

   - Show trends by drawing the outline of a periodic table. Use arrows to illustrate how a property changes as you move up and down as well as right and left along the periodic table.

   - Draw a periodic table and shade portions of it to show higher and lower values.

   - Construct a graph showing how properties change with atomic number.

3. Write a paragraph describing how certain properties of the elements change. Try comparing whether properties change in similar or different ways and give a reason, based on electron configurations, why this would be so.

Matter and Its Interactions

HS-PS1-2: Explaining Reactions

HS-PS1-2 Construct and revise an explanation for the outcome of a simple chemical reaction based on the outermost electron states of atoms, trends in the periodic table, and knowledge of the patterns of chemical properties.

Challenge Activity

Challenge: Use information from the periodic table to explain why certain chemical reactions occur.

The periodic table of the elements can appear to be a static resource. You might think that a simple alphabetical listing of the elements, giving pertinent information such as average atomic masses and atomic numbers, would serve the same purpose. To chemists, however, the periodic table is a powerful tool, one they use to determine the chemical formulas of compounds and the products of chemical reactions, such as those shown below.

The reaction of vinegar and baking soda is evidenced by the production of bubbles of carbon dioxide gas.

When water solutions of ammonium sulfide and cadmium nitrate are combined, the yellow precipitate cadmium sulfide forms.

For example, if you know that magnesium (Mg) combines with chlorine (Cl) to form magnesium chloride ($MgCl_2$), a quick look at the periodic table will tell you that calcium (Ca) and beryllium (Be) also react with chlorine to form calcium chloride ($CaCl_2$) and beryllium chloride ($BeCl_2$). Similarly, magnesium and iodine (I) form magnesium iodide (MgI_2). You can determine all these compounds quickly because atoms in each come from the same two groups in the periodic table: the alkaline earth metals and the halogens. Because the elements in each group have similar electron configurations, you can assume that any two elements from those groups will combine in a similar way.

The arrangement of the periodic table also tells you which elements are more reactive than others. In general, elements at the top left of the table are more reactive than elements at the bottom right. For example, lithium (Li) is extremely reactive, while lead (Pb) is not. Experimentation has led to the development of an activity series of the elements, an empirical tool chemists use to predict the products of a chemical reaction. It ranks elements according to their reactivity, with the more reactive elements appearing at the top. For example, lithium is the top metal in the activity series, so you can expect that it would replace any other element below it in a compound. You can find a copy of the activity series in Section 8.3 of the *Student Edition.*

Although periodic trends such as ionization energy and electron affinity play a role in chemical reactions, those values are often determined when the element is a gas. An activity series is generated using substances in solution. Other factors, such as free energy change, are considered when determining an element's place in the activity series. As an example, you might expect sodium (Na) to be more reactive than lithium because it has lower ionization energy and loses electrons more readily, but that is not the case.

In this Challenge Activity, you are not being asked to predict chemical reactions, but to explain why a given chemical reaction occurs. You will need to consider the characteristics of the reactants and other compounds you know about to determine which products will form.

MEET THE CHALLENGE

1. Review *Student Edition* Section 8.1, Describing Chemical Reactions, and Section 8.2, Types of Chemical Reactions. These sections outline the rules for writing chemical reactions and the types of chemical reactions that occur. For each section, complete the Formative Assessment and Chapter Review questions as directed by your teacher.

2. Review *Student Edition* Section 8.3, Activity Series of the Elements. Learn how to use the activity series to determine what substances will displace others in a chemical reaction. Complete the Formative Assessment and Chapter Review questions as directed by your teacher.

3. Complete the tasks detailed in the Documentation section.

TIP

To predict the success of chemical reactions, refer to The Periodic Table of the Elements (*Student Edition* Section 5.2, Figure 2.3) and the Activity Series of the Elements (*Student Edition* Section 8.3, Figure 3.1).

DOCUMENTATION

1. **Predict** Consider the formula for sodium chloride, NaCl. Write the formulas for at least four other compounds that you can assume exist based on the formula for NaCl. How are you able to predict that these compounds exist?

2. **Explain** Examine the chemical reactions presented. Using the periodic table and activity series, determine whether each chemical reaction would occur. Explain your choice.

   a. $2HCl + Zn \rightarrow ZnCl_2 + H_2$

   b. $2Al + 3ZnCl_2 \rightarrow 3Zn + 2AlCl_3$

   c. $KCl + Na \rightarrow NaCl + K$

   d. $Au + O_2 \rightarrow Au_2O$

   e. $2Ca + O_2 \rightarrow 2CaO$

3. **Revise** Check the explanations you provided in Item 2 and perform additional research. Revise your explanations with additional detail or change any explanation that is incorrect.

HS-PS1-3: Strength of Electrical Forces Between Particles

HS-PS1-3 Plan and conduct an investigation to gather evidence to compare the structure of substances at the bulk scale to infer the strength of electrical forces between particles.

Challenge Activity

Challenge: Observe the properties of substances at the bulk scale to determine the strength of the electrical forces between the particles that make up that substance.

The properties of substances depend not only on the elements of which they are made but to a large extent also on the types of chemical bonds that hold the atoms of those elements together. If something is durable at the bulk scale, you can be fairly certain that the chemical bonds holding its molecules together are durable as well.

Chemical bonds are electrical in nature. Chemists measure a bond's strength with reference to the electronegativity of the atoms involved. *Electronegativity* is a measure of an atom's ability to attract electrons. The greater the difference in electronegativities between two atoms, the stronger the chemical bond is between those two atoms, as illustrated below.

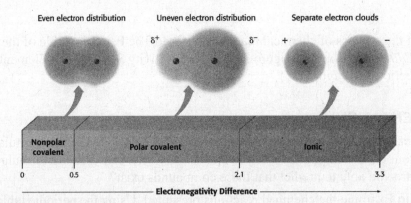

Predicting Bond Character from Electronegativity Differences

Even electron distribution | Uneven electron distribution | Separate electron clouds

δ^+ δ^- +   −

Nonpolar covalent | Polar covalent | Ionic

0   0.5   2.1   3.3

← Electronegativity Difference →

Chemical bonds in the traditional sense, however, are not the only forces that contribute to the bulk properties of materials. This is because the electronegativities of two chemically bonded atoms rarely balance each other out completely, unless two atoms forming a chemical bond are atoms of the same element. The result is that most molecules contain atoms that possess some residual charge. The residual charges on the atoms of one molecule will attract and repel similar and opposite charges on other molecules and thereby affect the overall properties of the substance at the bulk scale. One liquid boils at a higher or lower temperature than another, mostly because of the relative strengths of these intermolecular forces between their molecules.

In this Challenge Activity, you will examine various properties of substances and use your observations to infer the strengths of the chemical bonds holding the atoms in their molecules together. With the aid of computer simulations, you will also examine the relative strengths of intermolecular forces between the molecules of various substances and make inferences regarding how these affect the bulk properties of these substances.

HS-PS1-3: Strength of Electrical Forces Between Particles *continued*

MATERIALS

- materials list in Section 6.4 Lab: Types of Bonding in Solids
- PhET simulation, Molecule Polarity
- *Student Edition*

SAFETY

Wear goggles to perform this lab.

MEET THE CHALLENGE

1. Complete the Section 6.4 Core Skill Lab: Types of Bonding in Solids. Fill out the data table provided in the lab, and answer the analysis questions as directed by your teacher.

2. Using your Internet browser, search for "PhET simulation Molecule Polarity." Once in the simulation, go to the tab labeled Real Molecules. Using the dropdown menu, go to the molecules water, H_2O, hydrogen fluoride, HF, methane, CH_4, and ammonia, NH_3. In the View option box, click on the options to view Molecular Dipole and Partial Charges for each molecule. Examine any other of the other options and molecules as time allows. Record your observations about each molecule.

3. Next go to either the Two Atoms or Three Atoms tab and examine how the molecular dipole changes as you change the relative value of each atom's electronegativity.

4. Answer the questions in the Documentation section to complete the activity.

TIP

Materials have many other properties than those examined in the activity. Look at different materials around you and make conjectures about the properties of the molecules that compose them. Consult the *Student Edition* or other sources to see if your conjectures are correct.

DOCUMENTATION

1. What type of chemical bond tends to be the strongest? How is this reflected in the properties you observed for polar compounds in the lab activity?

2. Sugar and salt dissolve in water, but sand (silica) does not. Why?

3. After examining the molecules in the PhET simulation, which one would you suspect to have the highest boiling point? Which one do you suspect to have the lowest? Consult the *Student Edition* or other reliable sources to check your predictions.

4. Viscosity is a property of a liquid often referred to as "resistance to flow." Motor oil is a very viscous substance composed of nonpolar covalent molecules. Why would motor oil be viscous?

5. Nylon is a synthetic fabric known for its flexibility and ability to stretch. Based on this information, describe the kind of molecules you would expect to compose nylon.

Matter and Its Interactions

HS-PS1-4: Reaction Energy and Thermochemistry

HS-PS1-4 Develop a model to illustrate that the release or absorption of energy from a chemical reaction system depends upon the changes in total bond energy.

Challenge Activity

Challenge: Learn about energy transfer and enthalpy of reaction using models of exothermic and endothermic reactions. Use Hess's law to demonstrate mathematically that the overall enthalpy change of a reaction is equal to the sum of enthalpy changes for the individual steps in the process as a result of changes in the system's total bond energy.

Bond energy is the energy required to break a chemical bond and form neutral isolated atoms. A *chemical reaction* is the process of changing one or more substances into one or more different substances through the breaking and/or creation of such bonds. This rearrangement of bonds will lead to an overall change in the amount of energy stored within the substances, resulting in energy being either released or absorbed over the course of a reaction.

Thermochemistry is the study of the transfers of energy that accompany chemical reactions and physical changes. The amount of energy released or absorbed as heat by a reaction system at constant pressure is known as the *enthalpy of reaction*. This value represents the change in overall bond energy between the reactants and the products. Reactions that release energy are called *exothermic reactions*, whereas reactions that absorb energy are called *endothermic*, as illustrated in the graphs below.

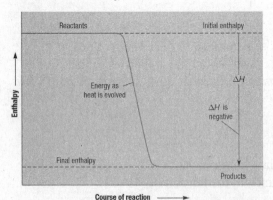

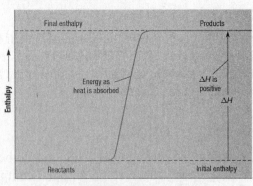

The enthalpy of a reaction can be modeled using a thermochemical equation. Because the enthalpy of a reaction is dependent on the changes in bond energy between the reactants and the products, thermochemical equations can be rearranged and added to calculate reaction enthalpy values for new reactions, as long as the reactants and the products are balanced. Hess's law states that the overall enthalpy of change in a reaction is equal to the sum of enthalpy changes for the individual steps in the process. No matter what steps occur in the process of changing one or more substances into one or more other substances, as long as the reactants and the products are the same, the overall change in enthalpy is always the same. This is in keeping with the laws of conservation of energy and conservation of mass.

| HS-PS1-4: Reaction Energy and Thermochemistry *continued*

In this Challenge Activity, you will examine how the enthalpy of a reaction can be modeled by thermochemical equations. You will apply the mathematical analysis of reaction enthalpies to the construction of a model that represents changes in bond energies over the course of a reaction.

MATERIALS

• additional materials as outlined in laboratory procedures

• *Student Edition*

MEET THE CHALLENGE

1. Read the sections of the *Student Edition* that explain enthalpy of reactions, thermochemical equations, and Hess's law, particularly sections 16.1 and 16.2. Complete any section assessment and chapter review questions as assigned by your teacher. Note that Hess's law states that the enthalpy difference between reactants and products is independent of the reaction pathway, meaning the enthalpy of reaction can be calculated by combining a variety of separate reactions to model the same reactants and end products.

2. Complete the laboratory investigation determining the heat of reaction of NaOH and HCl in the Section 16.1 Core Skill Lab: Calorimetry and Hess's Law. Record the data as indicated in the investigation procedure, and answer the Analysis questions.

TIPS

• Remember that thermochemical equations represent numbers of moles (not numbers of molecules), which allows you to write fractional values for your coefficients when determining formation reactions and balancing equations.

• Although basic laboratory calorimetry calculations may treat the calorimeter as a perfect insulator by assuming no energy was lost to the environment outside of the system, small amounts of energy will always be transferred between the calorimeter and its surroundings. For this reason, the heat capacity of the calorimeter itself is often also included in calorimetric enthalpy calculations.

DOCUMENTATION

1. **Analyzing and Interpreting Data** Report the data from the Section 16.1 Core Skill Lab: Calorimetry and Hess's Law. Provide your answers to the questions in the Analysis portion of the lab activity.

   • Show your calculations for the enthalpy of reaction for HCl(*aq*) and NaOH(*s*), including the results from both the direct and the indirect measurements you performed.

   • For each reaction, use your reported values to create a model diagram of the reaction pathway, showing enthalpy over the course of the reaction.

2. **Models** Design a theoretical reaction that can be modeled with a series of subreactions based on the combustion and formation reactions listed in *Student Edition* Appendix Tables B-5 and B-14.

   • Write a balanced formula equation for the model reaction and each subreaction.

   • Use Hess's law to calculate the overall enthalpy of the model reaction based on the combined enthalpies of the subreactions.

   • Again, create a model diagram of each reaction pathway, showing enthalpy over the course of the reaction.

Matter and Its Interactions

HS-PS1-5: Reaction Kinetics

HS-PS1-5 Apply scientific principles and evidence to provide an explanation about the effects of changing the temperature or concentration of the reacting particles on the rate at which a reaction occurs.

Challenge Activity

Challenge: Learn about reaction mechanisms and activation energies based on the kinetic-molecular theory of matter and collision theory. Study kinetic models of reaction pathways, and apply mathematical analysis to reaction rates using the rate law.

For reactions to occur between substances, their particles (molecules, atoms, or ions) must collide. To react, particles must have enough energy to transform into an activated complex upon collision. This minimum energy is called the *activation energy*. All reactions, even exothermic reactions, which release energy, require this initial input of energy to get started.

    Several factors can influence the frequency and efficiency of the collision of reactants. By changing the collision frequency, efficiency, or energy, the rate of the reaction will change. An increase in the temperature of a reaction system increases the average kinetic energy of the particles in a substance, resulting in a greater number of effective collisions when the substance is allowed to react with another substance. The increase in the number of effective collisions will increase the rate of the reaction. Additionally, increasing the concentration of reactants will increase the reaction rate as the frequency of effective collisions increases, as shown in the photo.

    Because many chemical reactions occur as a series of steps, the slowest step in the process determines the rate of the reaction. This step is known as the *rate-determining step*. Once you know the rate-determining step of a reaction, you can derive a rate law that relates the reaction rate to the concentration of the reactants. The rate law is applicable for a specific reaction at a given set of conditions and must be determined experimentally.

    In this Challenge Activity, you will examine how the rate of a reaction is determined by the kinetic behavior of its reactants. You will then use experimental data to demonstrate the effects of concentration on reaction rate.

MATERIALS

- additional materials as outlined in laboratory procedures
- *Student Edition*

SAFETY

Be sure to read and understand all safety precautions specified in the related laboratory procedure.

Pure oxygen has five times the concentration of oxygen molecules compared with air, so the charcoal will burn more intensely.

MEET THE CHALLENGE

1. Review Sections 17.1 and 17.2 of the *Student Edition*. These sections describe collision theory, reaction rates, and rate laws. Complete the assigned section assessments and chapter review questions as directed by your teacher. Note that the rate law accounts for the concentration of the reactants as well as the temperature (as part of the specific rate constant, k). If the temperature of the reaction increases, the value of k increases.

2. Complete the Section 17.2 Core Skill Lab: Rate of a Chemical Reaction. This laboratory investigation examines the effect of reactant concentration on the rate of reaction for $Na_2S_2O_5$ and KIO_3. Record the data as indicated in the investigation procedure, and complete items provided in the Analysis and Conclusions of the lab activity.

3. Perform the tasks described in the Documentation section.

TIPS

- The reactant orders described in a rate law must be determined experimentally. They are not always related to the coefficients of the balanced reaction equation because additional intermediate rate-determining steps may be involved in the reaction mechanism.

- Increasing the kinetic energy of reacting particles increases the frequency of the collisions as well as the collision energy, thereby increasing the odds that the particles will have effective collisions to form an activated complex.

DOCUMENTATION

1. **Analyzing and Interpreting Data** Report your data for the Section 17.2 Core Skill Lab: Rate of a Chemical Reaction, and provide your answers for the items described in the Analysis and Conclusions portions of the lab activity.

   - Show your calculations for determining the rate of the reaction for each concentration sample.

   - Propose a model reaction rate law for the reaction based on the changes in rate you observed in relation to concentration.

2. **Models** Suppose an exothermic reaction that involves reactants A and B is found to occur in the following one-step mechanism: $A + 3B \rightarrow AB_3$.

   - Design a model energy diagram for the reaction, and label ΔE, E_a, and E_a'.

   - Write a rate law for the reaction and predict the effect of tripling the concentration of either reactant.

   - Describe how increasing the temperature of the reaction relates to E_a and the specific rate constant k.

Matter and Its Interactions

HS-PS1-6: Equilibrium

HS-PS1-6 Refine the design of a chemical system by specifying a change in conditions that would produce increased amounts of products at equilibrium. *
*denotes the integration of traditional science content with an engineering practice

Challenge Activity

Challenge: Learn about chemical equilibrium, Le Châtelier's principle, and factors influencing the position of equilibrium. Apply this knowledge to an analysis of Haber process optimization.

A chemical reaction in which the products can react to re-form the reactants is called a reversible reaction. A reversible chemical reaction is in chemical equilibrium when the rate of its forward reaction equals the rate of its reverse reaction and the concentration of each product and reactant remains unchanged. Some reactions favor the products at equilibrium, meaning that at equilibrium there is a much higher concentration of products than reactants. However, the opposite is true for other reactions. The extent to which reactants are converted to products in a reversible equilibrium reaction is indicated by the numerical value of the reaction's equilibrium constant, K.

Because the concentration of reactants and products remains constant at equilibrium, a ratio of their concentrations will also remain constant. This ratio is the equilibrium constant, and for the general chemical equation $mA + nB \rightleftarrows xC + yD$ it is written as

$$K = \frac{[C]^x [D]^y}{[A]^m [B]^n}$$

where the brackets indicate the molar concentration of each substance and the superscripts are the coefficients of each substance in the balanced chemical equation. The equation for K is referred to as the chemical equilibrium expression; its numerical value must be obtained experimentally. A small value for K indicates that the forward reaction occurs only slightly before equilibrium is established and that the reactants are favored, while a large value for K indicates the reactants are largely converted to products at equilibrium. In heterogeneous reactions involving reactants and products in different phases, the concentrations of pure liquids and solids are not included in the equilibrium expression because they do not change. Note that the value of K applies only to the reaction at a specific temperature and will change with changes in temperature.

According to Le Châtelier's principle, if a system at equilibrium is subjected to a stress, the equilibrium is shifted in the direction that tends to relieve the stress. Changes in pressure, concentration, and temperature can shift the equilibrium of a system.

In this Challenge Activity, you will examine the production of ammonia through the Haber process. Ammonia synthesis is an exothermic reversible reaction described by the following equation: $N_2(g) + 3H_2(g) \rightleftarrows 2NH_3 + 92 \text{ kJ}$.

This forward reaction proceeds too slowly at low temperatures to be commercially useful. However, higher temperatures drive the equilibrium in the direction of the reactants, so other methods are required to obtain a satisfactory yield of ammonia. The use of a catalyst helps to speed up the reaction rate. As is often the case in industrial processes, chemists apply Le Châtelier's principle to shift the equilibrium to convert as much of the reactants as possible into products.

| HS-PS1-6: Equilibrium *continued*

MEET THE CHALLENGE

Using your understanding of equilibrium and Le Châtelier's principle, propose methods of refining the Haber process of ammonia production to produce increased amounts of product at equilibrium. Develop supporting materials that include visual models representing the principles behind your theoretical design solutions. Address the items in the Documentation section.

TIPS

- At the start of a chemical reaction, the concentration of the reactants is at a maximum, and the concentration of the products is zero. As the reaction progresses, the concentration of the reactants decreases, thereby decreasing the reaction rate of the forward reaction. Meanwhile, the concentration of the products increases, resulting in a simultaneous increase in the reaction rate of the reverse reaction. Equilibrium is reached when the two rates are equal.

- Adding an inert gas to the vessel for an equilibrium reaction involving gases will result in an increase in the total pressure of the system, but it does not change the partial pressures of the reaction gases. Therefore, increasing the pressure by adding a gas that is not a reactant or product does not affect the equilibrium position of the reaction system.

- Energy in the form of heat can be considered as if it were a reactant in the endothermic reaction direction or a product in the exothermic direction when determining the effect of temperature change on an equilibrium reaction.

DOCUMENTATION

1. **Designing Solutions** Report the results of your analysis of the Haber process. Include diagrams or other visual supplements to assist the evaluation of your findings.
   - Include the equation representing the chemical equilibrium expression for the reaction.
   - Discuss conditions engineers might adjust to shift equilibrium to favor the production of ammonia. Explain your rationale for each solution in detail.

2. **Arguing from Evidence** Discuss additional engineering considerations associated with the production process. Be certain to address the following features:
   - The addition of a catalyst to the system helps to assure the reaction takes place at a reasonable rate to be useful in production. Describe how a catalyst increases the rate of a reaction and why this helps the system reach equilibrium faster. How does the catalyst affect the equilibrium concentration of ammonia?
   - What other issues will engineers need to consider? How might safety or efficiency influence the final design of the production system?
   - Even at an optimized equilibrium, much of the input gases will remain unreacted. Ammonia condenses at a higher temperature than nitrogen gas and hydrogen gas. Describe how this characteristic can be used to benefit the production process.
   - The forward reaction is an exothermic process. Discuss how this energy output could be used as an asset in the process design.

Matter and Its Interactions

HS-PS1-7: Conservation of Mass

HS-PS1-7 Use mathematical representations to support the claim that atoms, and therefore mass, are conserved during a chemical reaction.

Challenge Activity

Challenge: Demonstrate the conservation of mass by comparing the mass of a system before and after reaction.

Calcium chloride and sodium bicarbonate are both chemical compounds used in in everyday applications. Calcium chloride is often used as a deicer on roads and to increase the mineral content of water to reduce erosion in swimming pools. Sodium bicarbonate, or baking soda, is regularly used as a leavening agent in baking as well as in other applications such as cleaning solutions and toothpastes. These two compounds react in an aqueous solution to form calcium carbonate, the primary component of chalk, which is also found in seashells, eggshells, and pearls, and is frequently used medicinally as an antacid. Additional products of the reaction are carbon dioxide gas and sodium chloride, or common table salt, in solution. In this Challenge Activity, you will mix known amounts of calcium chloride and sodium bicarbonate in water to create calcium carbonate, carbon dioxide, and sodium chloride.

MATERIALS

- balance
- calcium chloride, $CaCl_2$
- disposable plastic pipette
- graduated cylinder
- lab scoop
- phenol red indicator
- resealable plastic bag
- sodium bicarbonate, $NaHCO_3$
- water

SAFETY

- Always wear safety goggles and a lab apron to protect your eyes and clothing. If you get a chemical in your eyes, immediately flush the chemical out at the eyewash station while calling to your teacher. Know the locations of the emergency lab shower and the eyewash station and the procedures for using them.

- **Disposal** Clean your lab station. Clean all equipment and return it to its proper place. Dispose of chemicals and solutions in the containers designated by your teacher. Do not pour any chemicals down the drain or throw anything in the trash unless your teacher directs you to do so. Wash your hands thoroughly.

MEET THE CHALLENGE

1. Using the balance, measure 11 g of $CaCl_2$ and add it to the plastic bag.

2. Measure 7 g of $NaHCO_3$, and add it to the bag. Shake gently to mix.

3. Determine the mass of the bag and its contents. Record this value.

4. Using the graduated cylinder, measure 25 mL of water. Using the formula for the density of water, calculate the mass of the water.

5. Using the pipette, add 5 drops of phenol red indicator to the water.

6. Tip the bag sideways, and while holding the solids in the bottom corner, pour the liquid phenol red solution into the other corner. It is extremely important that you do not allow the solids to get wet at this point.

7. Carefully press the air out and reseal the bag. Hold the bag by the top, and let the contents mix.

8. Observe the reaction until it comes to a complete stop. Record your observations.

9. Again determine the mass of the bag and its contents. Record this value.

TIPS

- Thoroughly document all of the measurements you collect. Maintaining accurate data records will help you in analysis and evaluation of your procedure.

- Observe the system. Describe how it changes from the initial state to its final state. What evidence was there that a chemical reaction occurred?

- Is the system open or closed? What steps are you taking to control the system? How might you be better able to contain the system?

- The procedure calls for specific amounts of reactants to be added to the bag. Based on the reaction you observed, what issues might arise if you were to use larger amounts of reactants?

- Consider Avogadro's number and how it relates the mass of a substance to the number of particles in a mole of the substance. How does this help you relate the reaction that is occurring on a molecular scale to your observations on a macroscopic scale?

DOCUMENTATION

1. Report your observations. Write a balanced chemical equation for the reaction occurring in this activity. Demonstrate that the combined mass of the bag and the reactants should equal the combined mass of the bag and the products.

2. **Analyzing and Interpreting Data** Compare your measurements of the mass of the system before and after the reaction. Do they support the law of the conservation of mass? What explanations might account for any discrepancies? Determine the molar masses of $CaCl_2$ and $NaHCO_3$, and then calculate the number of moles of each reactant you used in the activity.

3. **Constructing Explanations** Based on the masses of the reactant you used and the balanced chemical equation you produced, which of the reactants was the limiting reagent in this reaction? Assuming 100% of the $NaHCO_3$ was used in the reaction, calculate the number of moles of each product you produced.

HS-PS1-8: Fission, Fusion, and Radioactive Decay

HS-PS1-8 Develop models to illustrate the changes in the composition of the nucleus of the atom and the energy released during the processes of fission, fusion, and radioactive decay.

Challenge Activity

Challenge: Using modeling clay, construct models of various atomic nuclei. Use these models to demonstrate the processes of fission, fusion, and radioactive decay.

Atoms are made of protons, neutrons, and electrons. Each particle has a specific mass. Each atom also has a specific mass. Interestingly, if you add the masses of all particles in an atom and compare the sum with the measured mass of the atom as a whole, you'd find that there is a difference. In fact, the measured mass of the atom is slightly less than the sum of the masses of the protons, neutrons, and electrons that compose it. This difference in mass, known as the mass defect, is related to the energy released during the atom's formation by Einstein's famous equation.

$$E = mc^2$$

The equation shows that energy is equal to mass times the square of the speed of light. When protons, neutrons, and electrons form atoms, part of their mass gets converted to energy known as the binding energy. The higher the binding energy of a nucleus, the more stable the nucleus is. The isotopes of the elements in the middle of the periodic table have the highest binding energy per nucleon, and tend to be stable. More massive elements, like uranium, have a lower binding energy per nucleon and tend to be unstable. Unstable nuclei tend to break apart spontaneously through radioactivity. The nuclei gain a higher binding energy per nucleon and become more stable.

In this Challenge Activity, you'll be using modeling clay to make models of atomic nuclei. You'll use these models to illustrate different types of radioactive decay, nuclear fission, and nuclear fusion. You'll then decide how to indicate the relative amounts of energy involved in each nuclear transformation. For example, you might accompany alpha decay (i.e., the ejection of two protons and two neutrons) with an audible "pop." You then might accompany nuclear fission (i.e., the splitting of a nucleus) with a more forceful "boom." You can decide the best method to use.

MATERIALS

- computer with Internet access (for research)
- modeling clay, at least two colors
- periodic table or other resource that provides masses for isotopes
- *Student Edition*

HS-PS1-8: Fission, Fusion, and Radioactive Decay *continued*

MEET THE CHALLENGE

1. Review *Student Edition* Sections 21.1, 21.2, and 21.4, as well as any other resources suggested by your teacher. Get to know how the nucleus changes during different types of radioactive decay, nuclear fission, and nuclear fusion. Get an idea of how much energy is released in each process.

2. Construct about 20 protons and 20 neutrons using different colors of modeling clay. You will use these to make your sample nuclei.

3. Complete the items detailed in the Documentation section.

TIP

Do not be concerned with making larger nuclei, like the uranium (U) nucleus. Use a sufficient number of protons and neutrons to illustrate the process, and be clear what nucleus or particle each model represents.

DOCUMENTATION

1. Using your protons and neutrons, model nuclear reactions. You can choose to model other specific reactions, but they should represent these processes.

   - **Alpha Decay** $^{235}_{92}U \rightarrow {}^{231}_{90}Th + {}^{4}_{2}He$

   - **Beta Decay** $^{14}_{6}C \rightarrow {}^{14}_{7}N + {}^{0}_{-1}\beta$

   - **Nuclear Fission** $^{235}_{92}U + {}^{1}_{0}n \rightarrow {}^{142}_{56}Ba + {}^{91}_{36}Kr + 3{}^{1}_{0}n$

   - **Nuclear Fusion** $^{3}_{1}H + {}^{2}_{1}H \rightarrow {}^{4}_{2}He + {}^{1}_{0}n$

   Provide your teacher with some evidence that you have completed the activity. Evidence could be your models, pictures of your models, or drawings of the various processes. Be sure your documentation includes information about the energy released in each process and a natural or artificial occurrence of each process.

2. Gamma radiation is another form of radioactive decay that releases only energy. Suggest a way of modeling gamma radiation.

3. Describe the amounts of energy released in each process, and explain what produces this energy.

4. With the amounts of energy released in each nuclear individual process being so small, why is nuclear energy so powerful?

5. List at least one natural or artificial occurrence of each process.

Motion and Stability: Forces and Interactions

HS-PS2-6: Chemical Bonding and Properties of Materials

HS-PS2-6 Communicate scientific and technical information about why the molecular-level structure is important in the functioning of designed materials.*

*denotes the integration of traditional science content with an engineering practice

Challenge Activity

Challenge: Learn about the properties that define different types of materials, and apply this information to identification of such characteristics in real-world objects.

A material's properties are determined by the types of bonding and intermolecular interactions associated with the arrangement of the material's atomic components.

Molecular compounds tend to melt at low temperatures because the forces of attraction between individual molecules are not very strong. Most molecular compounds are also completely gaseous at room temperature.

Ionic compounds tend to have higher melting and boiling points than molecular compounds, because strong attractive forces hold the ions together in a crystalline structure, which also causes them be brittle. In the solid state, the ions cannot move, so solid ionic compounds are not electric conductors. However, in the molten state, the ions can move freely to carry electric current, making them conductors. Many ionic compounds dissolve in water; because the ions are free to move in solution, these solutions are electric conductors.

Metallic bonding is characterized by a "sea" of delocalized electrons around the metal atoms, which are packed together in a crystal lattice. Because electrons can move freely within a metal, all metals are characterized by high electrical and thermal conductivity. Metals are also characterized by their malleability and ductility because planes of atoms can slide past one another without encountering resistance or breaking bonds.

Generally, solid materials are divided into two types: crystalline solids and amorphous solids. In crystalline solids, the particles are arranged in an orderly, geometric, repeating pattern, as shown below in the images of the crystal structure of sodium chloride. Amorphous solids consist of randomly arranged particles. Because amorphous solids do not have a distinct geometry, they can be molded into any shape. Additionally, crystalline solids generally do not flow, because their particles are held in relatively fixed positions.

Crystal Structure of NaCl Two models of the crystal structure of sodium chloride are shown.

—Cl⁻
—Na⁺

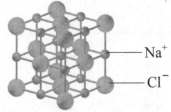

—Na⁺

—Cl⁻

(a) To illustrate the ions' actual arrangement, the sodium and chloride ions are shown with their electron clouds just touching.

(b) In an expanded view, the distances between ions have been exaggerated in order to clarify the positioning of the ions in the structure.

Crystalline solids have a definite melting point, the temperature at which the kinetic energies of the particles overcome the attractive forces holding them together. Amorphous solids, such as glass and plastic (a type of polymer), do not have definite melting points but have the ability to flow over a range of temperatures.

Polymers are large molecules made of many small units (monomers) joined through organic reactions. Polymers are generally very strong and lightweight, and can be arranged amorphously or in crystalline structures, making them useful in a variety of engineering applications.

In this Challenge Activity, you will examine the properties and behaviors inherent to the molecular structures of different materials. Scientists and engineers use these characteristics every day as they design, manufacture, and operate machines, processes, and systems. The materials you come into contact with and use on a daily basis are the product of thoughtful engineering and careful consideration of their molecular properties.

MEET THE CHALLENGE

1. Complete the Section 6.4 Core Skill Lab: Types of Bonding in Solids. In this lab, you will examine the physical properties of different solids. Record the data as indicated in the procedure, and answer the Analysis and Conclusions portions of the lab assessment.

2. Consider the properties of different materials and how those properties affect use of the materials. Describe some everyday substances and the molecular structures that define their properties. Specify substances that contain ionic, covalent, and metallic bonds and identify the characteristics associated with each type of substance. Address the items in the Documentation section.

TIPS

• Lattice energy is the energy released when an ionic crystalline compound is formed from gaseous ions. This is the amount of energy that must be overcome for an ionic compound to dissolve in water.

• Metals contain many orbitals separated by extremely small energy differences, allowing them to absorb a wide range of light frequencies. This re-radiated light is responsible for a metal's "metallic" appearance.

DOCUMENTATION

1. **Analyzing and Interpreting Data** Record your data from the Types of Bonding in Solids lab. Include your answers to the questions in the Analysis and Conclusions sections.

2. **Investigation** Report on each of the following:

   • Identify an everyday substance that contains ionic bonds. Explain your reasoning, and describe how the properties of ionic bonds affect how the material is used.

   • Identify an everyday substance that contains molecular bonds. Explain your reasoning, and describe how the properties of molecular bonds affect how the material is used.

   • Identify an everyday substance that contains metallic bonds. Explain your reasoning, and describe how the properties of metallic bonds affect how the material is used.

   • Identify an object that is a crystalline solid. Describe how the properties of crystalline solids suit the function of the material.

   • Identify an object that is an amorphous solid. Describe how the properties of amorphous solids suit the function of the material.

   • Identify an object that is a polymer. Describe how the properties of polymers suit the function of the material.

3. **Defining Problems and Designing Solutions** Consider how materials science is involved in the engineering of new technologies and products. Describe a situation in which the properties of a material have been used to refine or enhance its capabilities. Explain how these properties are related to the material's molecular structure.

Engineering Design

HS-ETS1-1: Criteria and Constraints

HS-ETS1-1 Analyze a major global challenge to specify qualitative and quantitative criteria and constraints for solutions that account for societal needs and wants.

Challenge Activity

Challenge: Make a guide to help someone think through the aspects of a decision about energy resources.

Energy resources—such as fossil fuels, solar energy, and nuclear energy—have associated costs, benefits, and risks. Costs include the amount of money paid, but also include something that is given up, lost, or damaged. During the Industrial Revolution (1760–1840), energy resources were used with only limited consideration of this second type of cost—resulting in pollution, the emission of greenhouse gases, and the depletion of nonrenewable resources. Today, there are international agreements that limit some uses to avoid these costs. However, the restrictions can make it more difficult for developing countries to become industrialized and to benefit from the resulting growth.

When an individual, community, country, or international group makes a decision about energy resources, others are affected. Some of the consequences might not be obvious, such as the costs or benefits that occur before the decision maker uses the energy. For example, the waste products of a power plant may not be obvious to someone using electrical power.

Explore a decision related to energy resources that a person or group might need to make, such as a city building and operating a nuclear power plant like the one modeled below. Identify the types of criteria and constraints that the decision maker should take into consideration. Think in particular about the role a chemist might play in helping to make these decisions. What aspects of the problems would a chemist concentrate on? How might a better knowledge of chemistry help others make the decision? Then make a guide to help someone consider the criteria and constraints specific to his or her decision.

Nuclear Power Plant

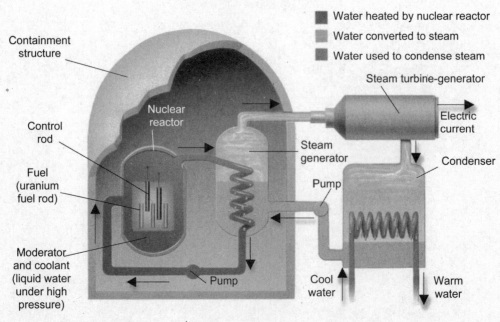

| HS-ETS1-1: Criteria and Constraints *continued*

MEET THE CHALLENGE

1. Choose a topic that interests you and involves energy resources. Also choose an audience—that is, the decision maker who will use the guide you make. Your focus might be very limited, such as an individual choosing a small appliance or deciding which grade of gasoline to use in an automobile. At the other extreme, you might address a global issue, such as how the use of some energy resources require environmental decisions that must be made by a group of international lawmakers.

2. Identify the main factors to consider in a decision involving energy resources. Remember, every decision has benefits and drawbacks. Coming to a decision is the process of getting the results you want with consequences you can accept. It may be helpful to exchange information with other students during this step. You may want to look up examples of energy resources and energy usage to ensure that you have identified most of the major issues. Don't limit your list to scientific issues. Include social, personal, aesthetic, and other issues. These issues may be important factors in a decision even if they can't be evaluated scientifically.

3. Recast your thoughts into criteria, constraints, and tradeoffs as a way to help guide decisions. Include lists, tables, flowcharts, or other means to help the decision maker gather information, review criteria and constraints, and evaluate the tradeoffs for a particular situation.

4. When you have a draft of your guide, exchange guides with other students and give peer reviews. Give feedback on the issues in the guide and also on its ease of use.

5. Improve your guide before submitting it to your teacher. Use your teacher's comments to improve your guide further if you wish to publish it.

DOCUMENTATION

1. Submit your guide. Be sure to identify the purpose and audience for your guide. Your teacher may ask for a copy of your guide in a format suited for adding comments.

2. Cite your sources and any resources that you recommend for the decision maker.

3. Explain how your guide is connected to global issues.

   - Note the ways in which your guide touches on the big issues related to energy resources.

   - Characterize the general human or societal need(s) that your guide reflects.

   - Consider how your guide might be related to other global issues, and then describe any strong relationships you find.

   Your teacher might specify the form for this information. If the choice is left to you, consider including it in an oral presentation of your guide to the class, producing it as a separate document, or integrating it into your guide. For example, you might help motivate a decision maker to reduce his or her ecological footprint or to minimize the release of greenhouse gases.

HS-ETS1-1: Criteria and Constraints *continued*

TIPS

You may wish to do Challenge steps 1 and 2 together. Understanding general issues related to energy resources may help you choose a topic.

Step 2 Suggestions

- You might start by listing general types of costs, benefits, and risks. For example, a school's costs for overhead lighting might include the initial installation, the replacement of bulbs, and the ongoing power consumption. The choice of lights might affect the school's reputation for environmental responsibility ("being green") or the resulting attractiveness of the space.

- You might think of pros and cons or of ways someone might oppose or support a particular choice. For example, pros and cons for different choices of overhead lighting might include the brightness and the color of the light, how hot the fixture gets, frequency of bulb replacement, and how well the light meets the lighting needs.

- You might imagine the qualities of a successful solution or consider intended and unintended consequences. Use any way of thinking that works for you. You might try several ways of thinking and/or several sources of information. Your results can be messy at this stage because you will organize them in step 3.

Limit the Problem

- If your topic is complex, keep your guide manageable by choosing just the top few issues that will affect the decision. You may also wish to put the most effort into the issues most closely related to the science you have been learning.

Criteria, Constraints, and Tradeoffs

- To identify criteria for an energy situation, record the needs and wants—the purposes filled by the use of energy resources.

- To identify constraints, record the limitations, such as a maximum budget or the desire to avoid the risk of harm.

- Look at the criteria and constraints together. Are any likely to be in conflict? Identify the tradeoffs that the decision maker should consider. Think about the form to use for this important part of your guide. Walk through a sample decision in your mind and think about whether lists, tables, flowcharts, or other devices would be helpful.

Ranking and Rating

- The decision maker might find it useful to rank items by importance. Recommend ranking items if you think it might be helpful

- As an alternative to ranking items, the decision maker might rate them, perhaps by classifying each as low, medium, or high priority. If applicable, try to formulate or find a rating scale that can be used to make comparisons for this particular set of criteria or constraints. Recommend rating items if you think it might be helpful.

HS-ETS1-1: Criteria and Constraints *continued*

Quantitative Measures and Sample Values

- It may be helpful for the decision maker to look at numerical values, such as available funds or cubic meters of a gas pollutant. He or she might consider relative values, such as the balance between price and income. In your guide, include ways for the decision maker to record and use these values. If you think it would be helpful, provide sample values, such as the current typical prices of two energy sources.

- Look at the sample values you might provide. Can you use them to save the decision maker the time of looking up actual values? For example, if the local costs of cooking with two energy sources are nearly the same, then the decision maker might use your sample values to decide to focus on a different issue. If the costs are very different, your sample values might allow the decision maker to make good-enough estimates rather than look up actual costs.

Priorities

- Help the decision maker be efficient. Perhaps the options for one tradeoff are likely to be close and difficult to evaluate. If a different tradeoff would be easier to evaluate and would produce a decision more quickly, then present this tradeoff first.

Format and Labels

- Choose a format for your guide that best suits the audience and your available technology. For example, if you wish to hand-draw a decision flowchart, or if your guide should be kept in a certain location, then you might design a physical booklet or pamphlet. If your recommendations include gathering information from online, your guide might be in the form of a webpage or other digital resource.

- Use clear labels to help ensure that the purpose of your guide will be clear to the intended audience.

Test and Iterate

- Imagine making the decision yourself and test the usefulness of your guide. Look for areas you can improve. Consider leaving out material that is less important.

HS-ETS1-2: Design a Lighting Plan

HS-ETS1-2 Design a solution to a complex real-world problem by breaking it down into smaller, more manageable problems that can be solved through engineering.

Challenge Activity

Challenge: Recommend a lighting plan for a school or a classroom.

Many schools rely on fluorescent tube lights, which are generally more efficient to run than incandescent lights. In the years since many schools were built, different forms of fluorescent lights, such as compact fluorescent light bulbs (CFLs), have become affordable. The lighting industry also has developed and continues to improve practical light-emitting diode (LED) bulbs. These lights use less energy to produce the same amount of light as incandescent lights. LED bulbs typically cost more but last longer. Sometimes new fixtures are required to accommodate new types of bulbs.

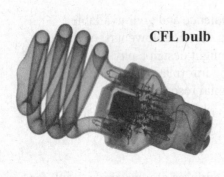

CFL bulb

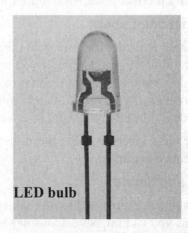

LED bulb

Recommend a lighting plan for your school or classroom. The ideal recommendation is environmentally responsible, assists in reducing eyestrain, and saves money in the short, medium, and long terms.

MEET THE CHALLENGE

1. Decide how to break down the problem into smaller pieces. You might evaluate the school or classroom's current lighting, decide on the most important changes, and then make recommendations of how and when to make those changes. Or you might start with an ideal lighting plan and look for ways to bring the existing system closer to the ideal. Think about these and other approaches, and then make a choice.

2. Plan your approach. What will you need for each step? What will you do? If a step depends on the results of previous steps, make contingency plans.

3. Your teacher will set expectations for this challenge. If you wish to exceed the expectations, such as by comparison shopping or by doing an experiment, then submit that part of your plan to your teacher for approval.

4. Implement your plan. Make adjustments as you go.

5. Gather your results and use them to make a recommendation.

DOCUMENTATION

1. Produce a summary of your recommendations. Put it in a form that would help someone implement your plan, such as a checklist or a diagram. If you recommend making the changes over time, then indicate this aspect in your summary, by labeling Phase 1 and Phase 2 changes, for example.

2. Provide a separate document with supporting details. Including the information and the sources you used. Explain the tradeoffs, and explain the reasoning for your choices. If any tradeoffs depend on future conditions, such as prices during a later phase, suggest a way to make the decision at the appropriate time. If any choices depend on personal preferences, provide a recommendation and also explain how the school officials could adjust your plan to suit different preferences.

TIPS

- You may find it useful to identify criteria and constraints for the desired lighting plan. These factors might include social or aesthetic considerations as well as financial costs and scientific factors. You might also wish to identify priorities, such as correcting problems, improving efficiency, or increasing environmental friendliness.

- If the time allowed for the challenge is limited, you may want to focus on just a few parts of the problem, such as improving the light in specific areas and reducing energy use. Other aspects of the lighting system can be left unchanged (rather than optimized).

- If you do this challenge as a full investigation, start by doing research. Guides to architectural design, interior design, home improvement, and commercial products can be good places to start. You might get a more complete picture if you consult several different types of sources.

- Photographs and other visuals may help you remember, describe, and communicate information about lighting. (Cite your sources.)

- Think about the purposes of the existing lights. Ambient lights provide general illumination. Task lights give more light for a particular purpose or in a particular area. Accent lights produce visual interest. You might identify other functions, such as safety lights, emergency lights, and warming lamps. These purposes result in different desirable characteristics.

- For task lighting, shadows and glare can be important factors. The placement and angle of the light can affect how functional it is. Sometimes diffusing the light or adding a second source can solve a problem.

- Too much light can sometimes cause more problems than too little light. (If you are familiar with the inverse-square law, you may be able to estimate when a small change in position is likely to have a big effect on outcome.)

- Decisions about the replacement of equipment often involve tradeoffs between the cost of the change and the savings in ongoing costs, such as energy use and bulb replacement. To make comparisons, it can be useful to calculate the time it would take for these two factors to be equal. The result is sometimes called the break-even point.

Lighting Systems

• There are several ways to use the idea of a system to help you devise a lighting plan. You might consider how the parts interact. You might think of input, output, controls, and feedback in terms of the light or in terms of the energy used.

• Think about how sunlight contributes to the lighting system. The direction and amount of sunlight change during the day and over the year.

• Windows, skylights, and the absence or presence of walls and other surfaces are ways of directing, reflecting, and diffusing light.

• Surfaces that reflect and diffuse light can change the effectiveness of lights. As a short test, watch as someone opens and closes a book in bright light. Observe how the light on the person changes as the book's pages reflect more light.

• Lights may interact with other systems. For example, lights may dim when certain equipment is in use, or lights may affect the temperature in an area.

Name _____ Class _____ Date _____

HS-ETS1-3: Tradeoffs

HS-ETS1-3 Evaluate a solution to a complex real-world problem based on prioritized criteria and trade-offs that account for a range of constraints, including cost, safety, reliability, and aesthetics, as well as possible social, cultural, and environmental impacts.

Challenge Activity

Challenge: Evaluate the use of an alternative energy source based on a set of criteria.

The sources of energy used in communities each have a combination of pros and cons. It is easy to compare two prices, but it is harder to compare different qualities, such as the relative values of human risk and environmental impact.

For this challenge, imagine that your team has been hired to advise a community council that is considering a proposal for the use of an alternative energy source, such as the one pictured below. The community's energy demands have been increasing. Members of the council have listed a variety of issues and negotiated some priorities. Your job is to evaluate the proposed energy source according to the list and then report your findings to the council.

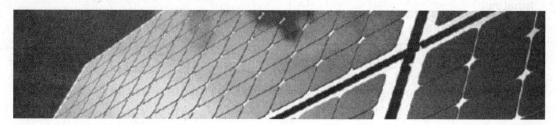

MEET THE CHALLENGE

Part 1: Set up the details of the challenge.

1. Your teacher will identify the community and the alternative energy source. Review the list of criteria and constraints and make the following adjustments:

   - Adjust the criteria and constraints to fit the community and the energy source.

   - You may divide items on the list into separate criteria and/or constraints.

   - You may propose adding or removing items, but ensure that the list represents the range of factors in HS-ETS1-3.

   - If the community is fictional, you may need to invent reasonable characteristics to fill in important details. For example, you may need to determine whether the new energy source needs to be reliable mostly for peak usage periods, at all ordinary times, or even in emergency conditions.

2. Choose a rating scale, such as 0 (not relevant) to 5 (very important). Roll a number cube or use another means to assign random values to each of the criteria and constraints below. You may then switch any two values to make the results more reasonable. You may make up to two additional switches.

3. Your teacher will tell you what type of report the council wants.

HS-ETS1-3: Tradeoffs *continued*

Part 2: Evaluate the proposed energy source and advise the council.

4. Identify the tradeoffs and evaluate the use of the energy source in the community.

5. Prepare and deliver your report for the council.

DOCUMENTATION

Your report for the council should meet the challenge in the format specified.

Criteria and Constraints

- The community needs more energy to meet increased demands reliably.
- The council's decision should be compatible with the values of the community.
- The decision should benefit members of the community equally.
- No one's safety should be put at risk.
- Risks to property, pets, plants, livestock, crops, and the environment should be minimized.
- The initial price should be reasonable.
- The ongoing price of the energy should be as low as possible.
- The service and maintenance costs should be as low as possible. (Assume a 30-year timeline.)
- Installation should be easy to achieve (such as by hiring a contractor).
- Installation should cause minimal disruption or destruction.
- Any structures needed for the storage or use of the energy should not have a negative impact on the community (by blocking traffic, spoiling views, lowering property values, etc.).
- The costs and risks should be fairly distributed among community members.
- Use of the energy should be easy.
- Use of the energy should not cause disruption—such as noise or odors—or destruction.
- Waste should be minimized.
- The decision should be environmentally responsible ("green").

HS-ETS1-3: Tradeoffs *continued*

TIPS

• Switch values in step 2 to make the results more reasonable. Consider whether the community is likely to consider some issues to be the most important, such as money, other costs, fairness, or responsibility. Be aware that council members often represent a range of viewpoints, some of which may conflict.

• State tradeoffs in useful ways. For example, a tradeoff between getting the highest possible quality and spending the least money can be expressed as "getting the best value for the money."

• If your evaluation shows that the proposed energy source would be a good solution, or shows that it would be a bad solution, say so in your report. Otherwise, identify the most important tradeoffs for the council to consider.

• Before delivering your report, try to see it as a council member would. Would you be satisfied with it?

• Consider working with other groups to critique each other's reports so that you can improve them before finalizing them.

Engineering Design

HS-ETS1-4: Model the Impact

HS-ETS1-4 Use a computer simulation to model the impact of proposed solutions to a complex real-world problem with numerous criteria and constraints on interactions within and between systems relevant to the problem.

Challenge Activity

Challenge: Explore one part of the complex issues of energy use and climate change by using a model to test proposed solutions.

The use of energy resources has complex effects on Earth's interacting spheres. For example, the extraction and burning of fossil fuels moves carbon from the geosphere to the atmosphere, typically in the form of carbon dioxide (CO_2). The production and use of biomass fuels moves carbon from the atmosphere to the biosphere and back again, although the system may also involve the use of other energy resources.

In the atmosphere, CO_2 acts as a greenhouse gas, absorbing and emitting radiation in a way that tends to keep energy in the Earth system, as shown in the graphic below. The resulting higher temperatures have many effects, such as causing ice to melt. Ice usually reflects sunlight more effectively than the ground or water do, so less ice means that more sunlight is absorbed into the Earth system. However, higher temperatures also cause more liquid water to evaporate, which can result in more clouds. Clouds reflect sunlight, so they prevent some solar energy from being absorbed by the Earth system. Clouds also reflect radiation from the ground, so they keep energy in the Earth system. Water vapor also acts as a greenhouse gas.

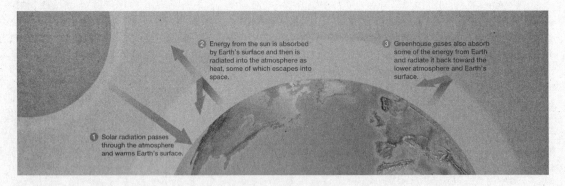

These feedback mechanisms are so complex that scientists can't make exact calculations for real-world situations. Instead, they make models with different simplifications and combine the effects of several models to make predictions. They might use one model to predict a change in temperature and a different model to explore how that change in temperature will affect sea level and coastlines. These models are often in the form of computer simulations.

In this Challenge Activity, you will use a computer simulation to model one aspect of a proposed solution for the use of energy resources. You will need to decide how to simplify the situation in order to use the model.

MATERIALS

- computer with an Internet connection
- note-taking and data-analysis tools, such as a spreadsheet or a physical notebook and graph paper

SAFETY

Use safe Internet practices. If you conduct an Internet search for a model, do not download or open files from unknown sources. Protect your personal information.

MEET THE CHALLENGE

You may wish to do steps 1 and 2 together so that your alternatives and your model are well matched.

1. Choose the computer model that you will use to explore an impact of energy use. Most of the tips below are written for a specific model, "The Greenhouse Effect." If you wish to use a different model, identify the model and what you will do differently, and then have your teacher review your plan.

2. Choose at least two alternative solutions involving energy resources that you can model. For this challenge, you may use unrealistic scenarios, such as changing all energy use to a specific type, or using half of one type and half of another. Use the current situation, or a simplification of it, for comparison with the two alternatives.

3. Translate each alternative in step 2 into a set of inputs for the computer model. You will need to make some assumptions or other simplifications (see the tips below). Test each set of inputs and record the results.

4. Use the model results to draw inferences about the solution(s).

DOCUMENTATION

1. Document your alternatives, your model, and the reasons for your choices.

2. Explain how the model inputs represent the alternatives. Identify the main simplifications that you made.

3. Present the model inputs and outputs (results) in an appropriate form. Make sure your audience can tell what's changing in the inputs and in the results.

4. Interpret the results and draw inferences. (You may wish to combine this information with #2 or with #3, if either makes sense for your work.)

5. You used a model to explore one part of a complex issue. Put your work in context by describing how the part you modeled relates to the issue as a whole.

| HS-ETS1-4: Model the Impact *continued*

TIPS

These tips assume the use of the computer simulation, "The Greenhouse Effect" (see below for details). If you use a different model, adapt the tips to your chosen model and your matching set of solutions.

Using "The Greenhouse Effect"

• Use a search engine to search for "PhET" and "Greenhouse Effect"—you'll need to find and run the simulation from the University of Colorado. Select Download or Run Now according to your teacher's directions. Within the simulation, use the "Greenhouse Effect" tab at the top.

Choosing and Analyzing Solutions

• Think about the current situation, in which much of the world's energy use comes from fossil fuels. As people use fossil fuels, CO_2 is added to the atmosphere. You might model just this part of the system by ignoring other greenhouse gases and by assuming that the amount of CO_2 will increase by a certain amount each year. (If you wish, use different simplifications.) Decide how to adjust the inputs of your model in order to simulate the current situation. Try it. Make adjustments as needed. Then record the set of inputs you plan to use to model the current situation.

• Decide whether to include cloud formation. For example, you might choose a temperature at which you'll add a cloud (increased evaporation would put water into the atmosphere). If the temperature in any of your tests drops below this temperature, you would remove the cloud (precipitation would remove water from the atmosphere). You can use this procedure, develop and use a different procedure, or ignore clouds.

• Think about a different energy resource. Does it produce greenhouse gases? Does it release them or water vapor into the atmosphere? If people used that energy resource instead of fossil fuels, would it change the rate at which material is added to the atmosphere (increase/decrease per year)? How would the total amount of material in the atmosphere be affected? Will it continue to change over time or become steady? Decide how to set and adjust the inputs to simulate the use of this energy resource. Record your reasoning as well as your decisions.

• Think about a third resource or a combination of resources. Decide how to set and adjust the inputs to simulate this energy solution.

• Test the model, and then decide whether you're satisfied with the way you're using the model. Adjust the simplifications or the way you set the model parameters, if you wish, but use the same approach for all three situations. Finalize your input sets.

Using the Model

- Test the model to learn what it can do. Identify the inputs and outputs. Look at the range of each, such as the maximum and minimum possible values. Identify some of the factors that are interrelated, such as factors in feedback loops. Think about the strengths and weaknesses of the model.

- For outputs, look at qualitative results and at sequences as well as final outcomes and measurements.

- Make at least one test to determine how best to record the model's results. Look at what varies the most and record these outputs. Look at readouts and at any visual or other qualitative depictions. How will you describe or account for them? What about outputs that change as the simulation runs—will the final outputs be enough, or will you need to describe intermediate outputs?

Getting the Most out of "The Greenhouse Effect"

- Inputs for this model include greenhouse gas concentration and cloudiness. However, the gas concentration is qualitative for most situations. The three color-coded settings show that the slider is not linear. The cloud variable also does not produce a linear effect, but you can estimate the amount of cloud cover for each setting.

- Before you decide on the inputs to keep constant, explore the range of each input. Try the preset inputs (Today, 1750, and Ice age) and different Greenhouse Gas Concentrations. Try varying the clouds, the thermometer setting, the photons, and the model speed. Record the possible ranges and your choices.

- For some inputs, you might want to test several options rather than keeping that input constant.

- The temperature readout is one output. However, you are not limited to temperature. You can pause the animation to sample the photons at different altitudes. To explore the radiation budget, you can watch the photons enter and leave at the top.

Presenting Results

- Choose a way to present the model inputs and outputs. For example, you might present the inputs that you kept constant in a table or a screen shot, and then use a table or graph to present the changes.

- If you prefer to think in scientific terms, you might treat the inputs that change as independent variables. However, your alternatives might not isolate the variables, as in a science experiment. For example, a change from gasoline to hydrogen fuel cells might stop the increase of CO_2 (a greenhouse gas) but would increase the amount of H_2O. Water vapor is a greenhouse gas and also affects cloud formation, so several variables would change.

- For this challenge, you had to make simplifications. Record the simplifications that you made. Discuss how those simplifications may have limited your results. For example, in the model, clouds are treated as an input. In the real world, water is part of several feedback loops. When clouds form, the water that condenses into cloud droplets or crystals is no longer acting as a greenhouse gas. The system is complicated and difficult to model, and so choosing the simplifications is part of the process of modeling.

Extensions

- Carbon-containing emissions are not the only factor in determining the amount of CO_2 in the atmosphere. Organisms on land and in the ocean remove CO_2 through photosynthesis and add CO_2 through respiration. The ocean can absorb and release CO_2, depending on temperature and on the amount already absorbed. Organisms in the ocean incorporate CO_2 into shells and other structures. But CO_2 makes water more acidic. Too much CO_2 can kill the organisms that remove CO_2 from the air and water. Temperature also affects the organisms. In other words, the feedback loops can be complex. Decide whether (and how) to take these effects into account in your model inputs. Simplify, but be aware of your simplifications.

- If you modeled clouds, think about extremes, such as consistent clouds or ice ages. You can use Earth's geological ages or other planets as ways of looking at these extremes. For example, the greenhouse effect on Venus is so strong that the planet is covered by clouds. Temperatures do not change much between day and night, and they are much more consistent from pole to equator than the temperatures on Earth. For a cold extreme, think about ways to use the clouds in the model to simulate ice cover.

- Think about more realistic models. One international goal is to make changes in human activity in order to keep global warming below 2°C (compared with the 1990 average). International agreements often center on reducing greenhouse gas emissions. Some agreements focus on a target date for the peak of greenhouse gas emissions, after which the rates will drop. However, reducing greenhouse emissions is not the same as reducing the total amount in the atmosphere. "The Greenhouse Effect" doesn't allow you to set numerical values for the greenhouse gases, but you might find a model suited to the modeling of international goals.

Engineering Design

Science is a way to study the physical world. Engineering design, in contrast, is a way to achieve practical ends. Both approaches often involve data, mathematics, and computational thinking. Both rely on evidence and often involve models. Both involve asking questions and solving problems. Scientific activities focus on asking questions to develop explanations, whereas engineering activities focus on defining problems to make changes.

USEFUL CONCEPTS IN ENGINEERING

In engineering, design is the purposeful or inventive arrangement of parts of details. It makes use of the ideas below. If any terms are unfamiliar, look over the appropriate section before reading about design cycles.

- criteria and constraints
- benefits, costs, and risks
- tradeoffs
- testing, troubleshooting, and redesigning
- systems: components, inputs, outputs, controls, and feedbacks

Engineering Design

ITERATIVE DESIGN CYCLES

Engineering design, like scientific inquiry, is based on a set of practices that are used in different ways. Engineers often use a method of repeated, or iterative, design cycles. The designs are possible solutions to the problem. During the iterations, a design is chosen, refined, and implemented as the solution. This method can be roughly divided into three types of activity:

- **Define** Determine the problem to be solved and its important details.
- **Develop** Plan ways to solve the problem—select or create designs.
- **Optimize** Test and evaluate the solutions and refine the most promising solution(s).

The first iteration, or design cycle, typically starts with a definition phase, followed by development, and then (usually) optimization. Additional cycles follow and may involve different sequences or combinations of these activities. For example, several cycles of optimizing might be followed by a new plan, a new definition of the problem, or separate cycles for additional problems. Sometimes an idea does not work out (or does not work out soon enough). In such a case, an engineer might develop new possible solutions or reconsider solutions that had been discarded. Sometimes the problem needs to be redefined. Sometimes a plan involves breaking the problem into smaller pieces. In the latter case, each of the smaller problems should be defined.

Use this guide as you define and solve an engineering design problem.

DEFINE THE PROBLEM

Think of your engineering problem as a situation that you want to change. When starting a new engineering project, first define the problem. For example, you might want to prepare food or plan a trip. When the problem has already been defined—perhaps from a previous design cycle—it is still a good practice to review the problem.

Engineering Design *continued*

You can define a problem by characterizing the criteria and constraints involved. Think about the conditions that a solution to the problem must meet to be successful, such as satisfying a group of specific needs and wants. Record those conditions as *criteria*. Think about any conditions that might limit or restrict a solution. Record these conditions as *constraints*. (You will find more detail in the section below about criteria and constraints.) For example, you might want to prepare food because a neighbor grew more vegetables than she could use and gave you a share of them. The criteria would include preparing the vegetables you now have. A constraint might be to use all of them while they are fresh.

You will use these criteria and constraints as you develop one or more designs to solve the problem. Some properties of a design, such as its price or the amount of time it takes to implement, may depend on the specific design. Your criteria may be to minimize these properties, to maximize them, or to match ideal values. Constraints can be requirements to stay within a range of values. Sometimes a constraint relates several properties, such as when the total price of several items must not exceed a budget. Whenever reasonable, quantify the criteria and constraints—describe them through numbers or comparisons.

At times, it is not possible for a solution to meet all of the criteria while staying within all of the constraints. At other times, you may need a solution so quickly that you cannot consider all of the criteria and constraints. In these cases, you may have to determine which conditions are more important than others, or what types of compromises you will accept. To identify these priorities, you might use labels such as *required* and *desired*, *acceptable* and *ideal*, or a numerical rating or ranking scale. You may find it useful to prioritize your criteria and constraints even if you think all of them can be met. Priorities can help you find a good solution faster by letting you focus on a simpler problem at first.

If a problem is complicated, you may be able to break it into smaller problems that you will solve separately. Sometimes you can separate small, connected problems by allowing each small problem to produce criteria or constraints for other small problems. As a result, you may need to solve some small problems before others.

As you define a problem, you may have to decide what to leave out. Real-world problems take place in larger systems. For example, a plan for lights for a school would likely involve the school's electrical wiring system, which could affect other electrical equipment. You can be distracted by all of the connections, and it is often wasteful to spell out all of the possible conditions. Instead, choose the conditions that are most important to test or confirm. Then group the rest of the connections by using a general statement or two, such as a constraint that the solution will not produce negative impacts. For the lighting-plan example, you might have a constraint that changes will not cause problems in the electrical system or other equipment.

DEVELOP A PLAN OR DESIGN

Research the problem and explore the possibilities. You may need to study the details of the problem or different aspects of the systems that are involved. As you generate possible solutions, you may need to find out even more specific information about the problem or the systems. You might even need to model or test the system to get necessary data. For example, you might map a route or use a trip calculator to determine the range of possibilities.

Review the solutions and processes that people have developed for other problems. It can be easier and less risky to adapt an existing solution than to invent a new solution. For example, it is usually easier to use or adapt a recipe than to invent one. Existing solutions have already been through cycles of optimization, so many of the component problems and issues have already been resolved. The effects of the solutions, including unintended consequences, are already known. You might be able to choose the best of several possible solutions, you might adjust one solution to suit your problem, or you might combine parts of different solutions.

Generate or find multiple solutions or approaches. Use your knowledge and your research to imagine possible solutions. The first idea is not necessarily the best idea, so try to ensure that you have explored a wide range of possibilities. Sometimes an unworkable idea can lead to a better idea. After you have generated a good set of ideas, use the criteria and constraints to evaluate the most promising ones. The use of criteria and constraints can help you be objective, especially when evaluating your own ideas.

Usually, designs alone do not provide enough information to produce the best solution—you need to test one or more solutions. Plan your approach for testing and optimizing. You may need to test and compare several solutions. You might find that one solution shows the most promise, but that you will need to test different settings or other details. The number of solutions and variations you test depends, in part, on the costs of each test. If testing is easy, you might be able to perform many tests. If testing has high costs or risks, you might use research, thought experiments, and calculations to reduce the choices. Or you might use a simple test or model to explore the feasibility of a solution or to gather data to adjust the properties of a solution.

OPTIMIZE THE SOLUTION(S)

You have many approaches available to find a good solution and adjust it to best suit your particular problem. You might test a real solution on the real situation, such as when you try a recipe or walk a planned route. This approach will usually give you the most reliable information, but it is not always reasonable to do. You may be able to test a sample of the solution, such as by cooking a small amount of food or by timing how long it takes you to walk a short distance. Often, you can test a solution by using one or more models. As you know, there are many different types of models to consider. You might combine sample data with a model. For example, you might use a friend's experience of walking your planned route, but adjust the time to reflect your own walking speed.

Test, evaluate, and refine your solution(s) iteratively. These cycles of optimizing your design are often when most of the work takes place. In the first cycle, you might narrow your choices to one main solution. In later cycles, you might refine different details of the design, such as the component pieces or the inputs to a system, to improve the performance or outcome of your solution. Tests and models can also help you clarify a problem or discover a new aspect to the problem. You may not be able to control as many of the factors as you would in a science experiment, but make your tests as systematic as you can.

| Engineering Design *continued*

Multiple Solutions

You might have several solutions to test, such as several cooking methods for a vegetable or several types of transportation for a trip. Apply each solution to your problem to find out how well it fits the criteria and constraints. Suppose you wanted to evaluate the amount of time needed for each solution. You might cook a sample of the vegetable using each method, or you might consult recipes to estimate the cooking time using each method. For a short trip, you might try each possible mode of transportation, or you might use an online trip planner to estimate the travel times.

These tests might also give you information about cost, ease of use, or other properties of the solutions. If one property is important enough to form the basis for a decision, you might make a single type of test. If several properties are important, you might need to make several types of tests.

Results can be complicated, such as when one solution is the fastest but a different solution costs the least money. You may need to make tradeoffs. You might find it helpful to rank or rate the time, money, and other factors. A chart that shows rankings or ratings may help you evaluate the solutions and see the possible tradeoffs clearly.

Details of a Solution

Sometimes, you need to test a solution just to see if it works. More often, though, you need to test different details of the solution. For example, you might test different power settings for microwave cooking or different times of day for a bus trip. In some cases, it works well to treat these variations as if they were different solutions, such as making the trip in rush hour or in the middle of the day. In other cases, you might explore how a factor affects the outcome (how two variables are related). For example, you might cook samples of food at low, medium, and high settings, evaluate the results, and estimate the best setting. You might then perform another set of tests at that setting and at settings slightly higher and slightly lower. In this way, you could optimize the power setting.

Troubleshooting

Sometimes a design does not work or is not reliable. You may need to try different ways to fix the difficulty or failure. You might study the difficulty as a new problem. These activities are called troubleshooting and are somewhat different from refining a design to improve it. You might find that the difficulty cannot be prevented, but that you can reduce the effects. You might also find that a design cannot be fixed or is not worth fixing. In such cases, plan a new solution or go back to your definition of the problem.

Unintended Consequences

Imagination and models can help you predict the outcomes of a solution but are not always complete enough. Solutions may have unplanned outcomes—good, bad, neutral, or mixed. When you are able to make a test of the real solution on the real problem, you are most likely to discover such unintended consequences. At times, you might test a solution or model in extreme conditions or continue the test until something breaks to determine the likely consequences of failure. You can also observe solutions similar to your solution to raise your awareness of possible outcomes. You might ask someone familiar with the problem to review your design or tests and identify possible consequences. You might adjust your criteria or constraints to take these effects into account.

Engineering Design Concepts
CRITERIA AND CONSTRAINTS

In science, you typically define a problem by identifying the variables and constants. In engineering, you typically define a problem by specifying the criteria and constraints. Criteria tell you the conditions for success, such as meeting specific needs or wants. Criteria might include a need to eat something nutritious and a wish for it to taste good, or a need to travel to a place for an event. Constraints tell you the limitations involved, such as cost, reliability, and the safety of people, property, and the environment. Criteria and constraints can go beyond science to include the interests of communities, cultural values, and aesthetic choices. They might include long-term effects as well as initial outcomes. They might require a solution to include ways to address any unfairness or reduce any harm.

Sometimes a condition can be stated as either a criterion or a constraint, such as the condition that food be nutritious. It may be easier to group criteria and constraints rather than to classify each condition as one or the other.

When you state criteria and constraints, think about how you will test solutions for success. When measurements, counts, or comparisons are useful, specify them. For example, you might specify that the price must be less than $10. But be ready to question and restate these conditions as you design solutions. If you obtain a discount or share expenses, the price might be greater than $10 while the amount you pay is less than $10.

BENEFITS, COSTS, AND RISKS

A *benefit* is an advantage resulting from a solution. A *cost* is a disadvantage and may include anything you give up or use up to achieve a goal. A *risk* is the possibility of suffering harm or loss—an uncertain cost. Some factors affect others. For example, a tightrope walker accepts the risk of falling, but a safety net can mitigate the cost of falling. Some factors may change over time. For example, small amounts of money, or of heavy metals in the body, may be negligible for any one event but may build up with repeated events. It may be difficult to predict some factors. Other factors may not be apparent until after a solution is implemented—a solution may have unintended consequences.

TRADEOFFS

In science, most of the problems you have encountered have exact solutions. In engineering, you instead seek to design the best solution for the criteria and constraints. You evaluate tradeoffs as one way of determining which solution is best.

A *tradeoff* is the exchange of one thing for another, such as when you give up a less-important feature for one that is more important. A tradeoff can also represent the balance among the needs and wishes of different people or groups. Tradeoffs usually apply to solutions and may reflect priorities. One solution might involve an increase in cost to improve time—that is, the solution would cost more but take less time. Another solution might do the opposite: it would cost less but take more time. You have to decide which tradeoffs to make. When you try to get the best value for the money, you are deciding on tradeoffs.

Engineering Design *continued*

TESTING, TROUBLESHOOTING, AND REDESIGNING

In science, you might isolate a single issue to understand it. In engineering, you must take into account the consequences of your design, even if you do not understand all of them. Testing and troubleshooting help engineers account for unknown factors. For example, engineers may perform tests and then use statistical methods to take into account the variation or uncertainty. To reduce risks, an engineer might add a margin of error or might design for more extreme conditions than those measured or expected. An engineer may use an estimate rather than an exact value if the result is good enough for a design. An exact value may be determined later or may not be needed.

As in science, engineering tests can involve real materials and situations, models of many types, and combinations of the two. However, engineering tests typically focus on comparing a solution with criteria and constraints and then making a small adjustment and retesting. Sometimes a different solution or a large adjustment is needed. These changes are part of redesigning and optimizing a solution.

Troubleshooting involves locating and eliminating sources of trouble, such as fixing a broken part. Sometimes the trouble cannot be located. For example, a failure may occur only sometimes, and the engineer may not be able to reproduce it reliably enough to study it. The engineer might adjust the design to affect the most likely cause or might take steps to mitigate the failure if it occurs again.

SYSTEMS: COMPONENTS, INPUTS, OUTPUTS, CONTROLS, FEEDBACKS

In science, you identify independent variables, dependent variables, and constants. You may have classified these factors as givens and unknowns. In engineering design, the situations are often complicated and it might not be possible to know all of the factors involved in a problem. For example, a variable might start out as independent but then be affected by other factors in a complex way.

An engineer may look at a problem in terms of a system or of interacting systems rather than in terms of variables. It is not always necessary to understand all of the details of a system. In many cases, you can treat a system as a "black box" by looking just at what goes into the system and what comes out, or the inputs and outputs. For example, you could view a factory as a black box that takes in raw materials and energy and puts out products and waste materials.

When you want to have a little more detail about a system, you might look at the parts of the system and at how they interact. Two useful ideas are controls and feedbacks.

Controls are a way of adjusting, on purpose, how the system works. Suppose you have a system in which a microphone is connected to a combined amplifier and speaker. The volume adjustment on the speaker is a control. You use it to adjust how much the system amplifies the sound—how much louder it makes the sound.

Feedbacks also adjust the system, but come from the system itself, usually from an output. If the sound from the speaker is picked up by the microphone, that sound is amplified and reproduced by the speaker. The resulting sound is also picked up by the microphone and increases the sound from the speaker. As a result, the sound grows louder and louder. Feedback is called positive when it tends to increase a change, as in this example. Negative feedback tends to reduce a change, or return a system to its previous condition. Negative feedback usually makes a system more stable because it opposes change. Where feedback exists, a variable can start out as independent but then become dependent as well.